A CENTURY OF STORMS

The Historical Impact of Hurricanes on Florida

By

Katrina Charles

Table of content

INTRODUCTION

Florida, a state known for its sandy shores, palm-fringed coastlines, and vibrant, sun-soaked cities, has also been a battleground against nature's fury. Hurricanes have left indelible marks on its landscape and its people. Each storm that sweeps across the state brings tales of destruction and resilience, of lives upended and rebuilt. Understanding the historical impact of these hurricanes is not just about recounting events; it's about appreciating the deep-seated legacy they've imprinted on Florida's identity. This book delves into a century of storms, mapping their trajectories and the stories that have emerged in their wake.

The Importance of Understanding Hurricanes in Florid a's History

Florida's history with hurricanes is as old as its settlement. These colo ssal storms have shaped the state's development, its economy, and eve n the psyche of its inhabitants. From the earliest recorded storms that battered the coasts of the Spanish colonies to the modernday hurrican es that challenge the most sophisticated of warning systems, each eve nt offers a lesson.

Recognizing the significance of hurricanes in Florida is crucial for sev eral reasons. First, hurricanes have been a constant threat, influencing settlement patterns, building codes, and urban planning. Early settlers

learned to build sturdy structures and develop warning systems, lesso
ns that have evolved over centuries. The Labor Day Hurricane of 193
5, for example, prompted major advancements in meteorology and em
ergency response. Understanding these historical events underscores t
he importance of preparedness and adaptation in contemporary times.

Second, hurricanes have played a substantial role in the economic narr
ative of Florida. The state's economy has been periodically battered b
y these storms, with industries such as agriculture, tourism, and real e
state often taking severe hits. The destruction wrought by Hurricane A
ndrew in 1992, one of the costliest hurricanes in U.S. history, necessit
ated a massive reconstruction effort that reshaped the economic lands
cape. Examining these economic impacts helps to elucidate how Flori
da's economy has adapted and rebounded in the face of such adversity
.

Moreover, hurricanes have a profound social and cultural impact on th
e communities they affect. They bring stories of loss, survival, and co
mmunity spirit to the forefront. The shared experience of weathering a
 hurricane fosters a unique sense of camaraderie among Floridians. St
ories from the 2004 hurricane season, when the state was hit by four
major hurricanes in quick succession, reveal the resilience and solidar
ity of its people. By understanding these cultural and social dimension
s, we gain insight into the collective Florida identity forged through s
hared hardship.

Finally, studying the historical impact of hurricanes in Florida is essen
tial in the context of climate change. As global temperatures rise, the f
requency and intensity of hurricanes are expected to increase, posing
new challenges for the state. Historical data provides a benchmark to
understand trends and develop more effective mitigation and adaptati
on strategies. For instance, the rebuilding of Homestead after Hurrica
ne Andrew serves as a case study in resilient infrastructure developme
nt, offering valuable lessons for future urban planning.

EARLY ENCOUNTERS

The Florida Peninsula, with its long coastline and strategic location ju tting into the warm waters of the Atlantic Ocean and Gulf of Mexico, has been a magnet for hurricanes for centuries. These powerful storms are as much a part of Florida's natural history as its swamps, beaches, and wildlife. Early settlers and indigenous tribes alike were aware of the destructive potential of these massive storms, learning to adapt to t heir inevitable impacts.

Hurricanes, or "tempests" as they were once called, have been docum ented in Florida as far back as the time of the Spanish explorers. Thes e early encounters between man and nature highlight the perpetual str uggle for survival in the face of these natural disasters.

Florida's First Documented Hurricanes

The first recorded hurricane in Florida's history struck on July 23, 155 9, when the Spanish fleet led by Tristan de Luna y Arellano was hit of f the coast of what is now Pensacola. The expedition was intended to establish one of the first European colonies in the New World, but the hurricane destroyed their ships, provisions, and hopes. This storm wa s a brutal introduction to the new environment for the Spanish settlers and set a precedent for the many hurricanes that would follow.

One of the earliest detailed accounts of a hurricane impacting Florida comes from the records of the Spanish missions. On September 5, 162 2, a hurricane devastated the Spanish treasure fleet, including the fam ed ship Nuestra Señora de Atocha, near the Florida Keys. The afterma th was catastrophic, with loss of life and treasure, embedding the fero city of these storms in the colonial psyche.

The Great Hurricane of 1780, though primarily devastating the Caribb ean, extended its wrath to the east coast of Florida. This hurricane was the deadliest in recorded history, causing tens of thousands of deaths across multiple territories. Its impact on Florida, although not as deadl y, demonstrated the reach and power of these storms.

Indigenous Peoples' Responses and Adaptations

Long before European settlers arrived, the indigenous peoples of Flori da had their ways of understanding and responding to hurricanes. The native tribes, such as the Calusa, Tequesta, and Timucua, viewed thes e storms through a lens of spirituality and practicality, interpreting the m as acts of gods or spirits, which required both respect and caution.

These tribes had intricate knowledge of the land and the sea, which w as crucial in their hurricane preparedness. They built their structures t o withstand high winds and flooding, often using materials that could be quickly repaired or replaced. The Calusa, for example, constructed

their homes on stilts to protect against storm surges, a practice that mo
dern architecture has revisited in flood-prone areas.

Indigenous people also developed early warning systems based on nat
ural indicators. They observed changes in animal behavior, sea pattern
s, and atmospheric conditions to predict approaching storms. This obs
ervational knowledge was passed down through generations, forming
a crucial part of their survival strategy.

Posthurricane survival strategies were also vital. Indigenous tribes had
 communal approaches to rebuilding and recovery, ensuring that resou
rces were shared, and support was provided to those in need. This sen
se of community resilience is echoed in modern disaster response effo
rts, underscoring the enduring importance of social cohesion in the fac
e of natural calamities.

20TH CENTURY STORMS

The 20th century was a transformative period for Florida, marked by r apid development and an everincreasing population. Yet, amidst the s unshine and growth, the state faced some of the most devastating hurr icanes in its history. These storms tested the resilience of its people an d reshaped cities. Among the most significant were the 1926 Miami H urricane, the Labor Day Hurricane of 1935, and Hurricane Donna in 1 960. Each left an indelible mark, not only on the landscape but also on the collective memory of Floridians.

The 1926 Miami Hurricane: A City Reborn

In September 1926, Miami was a burgeoning city with dreams of bec oming a major metropolis. The real estate boom was in full swing, an d the city was a magnet for new residents and investors. But all that o ptimism was shattered when a powerful hurricane, later known as the Great Miami Hurricane, made landfall. With winds estimated at 150 mph, it was a beast of a storm, unleashing a fury that the city was utte rly unprepared for.

As the eye of the hurricane passed over Miami, a deceptive calm desc ended. Many residents, unfamiliar with the phenomenon, ventured out side, believing the storm had passed. When the eyewall hit, they were caught off guard by the ferocious winds that followed. Buildings crum bled, streets flooded, and the death toll rose. The destruction was so e xtensive that the exact number of casualties is still unknown, with esti mates ranging from 300 to 800.

In the aftermath, Miami faced a massive rebuilding effort. The city's r eal estate boom collapsed, and many banks failed. But out of the rubbl e, a new, more resilient Miami emerged. Building codes were revised to better withstand future storms, and the city slowly rebuilt its infrast ructure. The disaster highlighted the need for better preparedness and reinforced the importance of community in times of crisis. Miami's re birth was not just physical but also psychological, as it transformed fr om a young city of dreams to a community forged in the crucible of a dversity.

The Labor Day Hurricane of 1935: Tragedy in the Keys

Almost a decade later, another hurricane would etch itself into the ann als of Florida's history, this time with even more deadly consequences . The Labor Day Hurricane of 1935 remains one of the most powerful and deadly hurricanes to ever strike the United States. With winds rea ching 185 mph, it devastated the Florida Keys, particularly the Upper Keys, with an intensity that few could have imagined.

On the evening of September 2, 1935, as the nation celebrated Labor Day, the hurricane made landfall. The Overseas Railroad, a vital link between the Keys and the mainland, was destroyed. Homes were swe pt away, and the storm surgesome 20 feet high in placesclaimed hundr eds of lives. Among the dead were more than 400 World War I vetera ns who had been working on construction projects in the Keys as part of the New Deal program. Their makeshift camps stood no chance ag ainst the storm's onslaught.

The aftermath was one of utter devastation. Bodies were strewn acros s the islands, and entire communities were obliterated. The federal go vernment responded by relocating the surviving veterans and their fa milies and launching a massive recovery and rebuilding effort. The hu rricane prompted significant changes in how the Keys were connected to the mainland, leading to the construction of a new Overseas Highw ay that would better withstand future storms. The tragedy underscored the vulnerability of the Keys and the need for improved hurricane for ecasting and response measures.

Hurricane Donna (1960): A Statewide Crisis

Hurricane Donna, which struck in September 1960, was a storm of im mense proportions, impacting the entire state of Florida and earning a notorious reputation for its erratic path and sustained intensity. Donna made landfall in the Florida Keys with winds of 140 mph, causing sig nificant destruction before traversing the entire length of the Florida p eninsula.

Unlike many hurricanes that lose strength quickly after landfall, Donn a maintained its ferocity, wreaking havoc as it moved northward. In th e Keys, homes were obliterated, and the storm surge left areas underw ater. As Donna continued its destructive path through Florida, it cause d widespread damage from the Everglades to Jacksonville. Cities like Fort Myers, Naples, and Tampa felt the full brunt of its power, with e xtensive flooding, wind damage, and power outages.

Hurricane Donna was notable not only for its intensity but also for the duration of its impact. It was the only hurricane in recorded history to affect every state on the U.S. East Coast from Florida to Maine, main taining hurricane-
force winds throughout its journey. In Florida, the damage was extens ive, with agricultural losses, particularly in the citrus industry, amount ing to millions of dollars.

The response to Donna highlighted the need for better emergency pla nning and infrastructure. The experience gained from this hurricane le d to improvements in building codes, emergency response protocols, a nd public awareness campaigns about hurricane preparedness. Donna' s legacy is a testament to the importance of learning from past storms to better prepare for future one.

THE MODERN ERA

In the modern era, hurricanes have become a central focus for communities across the world, particularly in regions prone to these destructive storms. Advances in technology and meteorology have allowed us to predict storms more accurately, but the sheer power and unpredictability of hurricanes remain significant challenges. Historically, hurricanes were seen as inevitable acts of nature, something to endure with basic preparation boarding up windows, securing loose items, and hoping for the best. But as the 20th century ended and the 21st began, society's approach to hurricanes evolved drastically. The advent of 24-hour news coverage and social media made the world acutely aware of the devastation these storms could bring.

In the United States, particularly in Florida, hurricanes have shaped policies, communities, and even cultures. The rise of climate change discussions has only added to the growing concern about these storms. Scientists debate how warmer ocean temperatures may intensify hurricanes, making them more frequent and more destructive. This era of heightened awareness has pushed governments to implement stricter building codes and enhanced disaster preparedness plans.

Despite these advancements, the emotional and physical toll of hurricanes hasn't changed much. Families still fear for their homes, livelihoods, and loved ones, and even with preparation, the unpredictability of a storm's path often leaves entire regions on edge. Every hurricane season brings a fresh wave of anxiety, along with memories of past storms that shaped communities and families forever.

Hurricane Andrew (1992): Redefining Disaster Preparedness

Hurricane Andrew, which struck South Florida in August 1992, was a defining moment in hurricane history. Before Andrew, few anticipated the level of devastation a Category 5 storm could unleash. Andrew changed that forever. With winds reaching up to 175 mph, the storm tore through Homestead, Florida, flattening entire neighborhoods and leaving a trail of destruction that took years to rebuild.

More than just a natural disaster, Andrew exposed serious flaws in disaster preparedness and response. At the time, building codes in South Florida were not strong enough to withstand the force of a storm like Andrew. Homes that were supposed to endure hurricanes crumbled under the intense winds. In the aftermath, it became clear that change was necessary.

In response, Florida enacted some of the most stringent building codes in the country. Structures built after Andrew were required to be more resilient, with stronger roofs, impact-resistant windows, and more robust structural reinforcements. These changes were a direct result of the devastation left in Andrew's wake, and they have since been credited with preventing similar destruction in later hurricanes.

However, beyond infrastructure, Andrew also redefined how communities prepare for and respond to hurricanes. Emergency management teams began emphasizing early evacuations, clearer communication, and better coordination between state and federal agencies. The lessons learned from Andrew not only shaped Florida but also influenced national disaster preparedness policies. Andrew served as a grim reminder of nature's fury but also sparked a much-needed overhaul in how we prepare for hurricanes today.

The 2004 Quartet: Charley, Frances, Ivan, and Jeanne

If Hurricane Andrew taught us to rethink building codes and preparedness, the 2004 hurricane season showed us just how relentless nature could be. In what seemed like an endless assault, Florida was hit by four major hurricanes Charley, Frances, Ivan, and Jeanne in a span of just six weeks. Each storm had its unique path of destruction, and by the time Jeanne struck in late September, many Floridians were left wondering if it would ever end.

Hurricane Charley, the first of the quartet, struck the southwestern coast of Florida in mid-August, taking an unexpected turn and slamming into Punta Gorda. It was the strongest of the four, with winds up to 150 mph. Charley's speed meant it was over relatively quickly, but not before causing extensive damage. Next came Frances, a slower-moving storm that covered nearly the entire state in heavy rain and flooding, exacerbating the damage caused by Charley. Ivan followed soon after, carving a path through the Caribbean before making landfall in the Florida Panhandle and Alabama. Ivan's strength and size were immense, bringing destruction far inland. Finally, Jeanne hit in late September, retracing much of Frances' path and leaving even more flooding in her wake.

The economic and emotional toll of four hurricanes in such quick succession was enormous. Many people had barely begun cleaning up from one storm before another was on its way. Insurance claims skyrocketed, homes were destroyed, and the power grid was strained to its limits. Yet, these back-to-back disasters also showcased the resilience of the communities affected. People came together, helping one another, sharing supplies, and offering shelter.

Despite the chaos, the lessons from Hurricane Andrew helped mitigate some of the destruction. Stronger buildings fared better, and emergency services were quicker and more organized in their response. Still, the 2004 season was a brutal reminder that even the best preparations can be overwhelmed by nature's power.

The Economic Aftermath: Tourism, Real Estate, and Insurance

The economic aftermath of hurricanes is often felt long after the storm has passed. In Florida, an economy heavily reliant on tourism, real estate, and agriculture, the effects of major hurricanes are profound and wide-ranging. After Hurricane Andrew, and even more so after the 2004 hurricane season, these industries faced significant challenges.

Tourism, the lifeblood of Florida's economy, is particularly vulnerable to hurricanes. Images of destruction on the news can dissuade travelers for months, even if popular tourist destinations aren't directly affected. After the 2004 hurricanes, many hotels and resorts were closed for repairs, leading to lost revenue. However, Florida's tourism industry is resilient, and recovery efforts are often swift. The state's natural beauty and theme parks remain a strong draw, even after devastating storms.

Real estate, too, takes a hit. In the immediate aftermath of a hurricane, home values in hard-hit areas tend to drop. Properties are either damaged or viewed as risky investments due to their location in hurricane-prone areas. Yet, over time, these areas often bounce back as repairs are made and new, more resilient homes are built. In the long term, hurricanes can lead to stronger, safer communities as outdated homes are replaced with those built to stricter codes.

Perhaps the industry most impacted by hurricanes is insurance. After the 2004 hurricane season, insurance companies faced an onslaught of claims, leading to skyrocketing premiums in the years that followed. Some companies even pulled out of the Florida market altogether, leaving homeowners with fewer options and higher costs. The insurance landscape in hurricane-prone areas remains challenging, as companies try to balance risk with profitability.

Hurricanes are a fact of life in Florida and other coastal regions, but with each storm, new lessons are learned, and communities continue to adapt. From the devastation of Andrew to the relentless quartet of 2004, Floridians have proven time and again their resilience in the face of nature's fury.

CLIMATE CHANGE AND ITS IMPL ICATIONS

As the 21st century advances, the conversation surrounding climate c hange has become more urgent and essential. The implications of a w arming planet are far-
reaching, affecting every corner of the globe, but few places feel its i mpact as profoundly as Florida. Situated at the crossroads of tropical weather systems and boasting a vast coastline, Florida stands on the fr ontline of climate change, grappling with rising seas, warming waters, and increasingly unpredictable weather patterns. Understanding these changes and developing strategies to mitigate their effects is crucial f or the state's future resilience.

Rising Seas and Warming Waters: Future Hurricane Pa tterns

One of the most immediate and visible effects of climate change in Fl orida is sea level rise. Over the past century, sea levels have risen by a bout 8 inches globally, and projections suggest an increase of up to se veral feet by the end of this century. For a state like Florida, where m uch of the land is just a few feet above sea level, this poses a significa nt threat. Coastal erosion, increased flooding, and the loss of critical h abitats are all part of the grim reality that Floridians must face.

Warming waters in the Atlantic and Gulf of Mexico are another seriou
s concern. Hurricanes draw their energy from warm ocean water, and
as sea temperatures rise, the potential for stronger and more destructiv
e hurricanes increases. Historically, hurricane season peaks in late su
mmer when water temperatures are at their highest, but with the overa
ll warming trend, the window for hurricane formation may extend, an
d the intensity of these storms could grow more severe.

In recent years, we've seen hurricanes rapidly intensify as they approa
ch the coast, a phenomenon closely linked to warmer waters. Hurrican
es like Irma in 2017 and Michael in 2018 underwent rapid intensificat
ion, catching many by surprise and overwhelming preparedness effort
s. This pattern is likely to become more common, making it imperativ
e for forecasting models to evolve and for communities to remain vigi
lant.

Additionally, rising sea levels contribute to higher storm surges. Whe
n a hurricane pushes water onshore, higher baseline sea levels mean t
he surge can penetrate further inland, causing more severe flooding an
d damage. Urban areas, especially those built on low-
lying land, are particularly vulnerable. Cities like Miami and Tampa a
re investing heavily in flood defense systems, but the increasing frequ
ency of these events demands continuous innovation and adaptation.

Mitigation and Adaptation Strategies

Addressing the challenges posed by climate change requires a multi-faceted approach, combining mitigation efforts to reduce greenhouse gas emissions with adaptation strategies to manage the impacts that are already inevitable.

Mitigation

Reducing emissions is the cornerstone of any effective climate change strategy. For Florida, this means transitioning to renewable energy sources like solar and wind, which are abundant in the Sunshine State. Investing in energy efficiency, promoting sustainable transportation options, and encouraging conservation efforts can all contribute to lowering the state's carbon footprint.

Policy measures also play a crucial role. Implementing stricter emissions standards for vehicles, supporting the development of green infrastructure, and participating in regional and national climate initiatives can drive significant progress. Additionally, preserving and restoring natural carbon sinks, such as wetlands and mangroves, can help sequester carbon dioxide from the atmosphere while providing critical habitat for wildlife and acting as natural buffers against storm surges.

Moreover, technological advancements offer promising avenues for reducing emissions. Innovations in battery storage, smart grid systems, and energy-

efficient building materials can all contribute to a more sustainable an
d resilient energy infrastructure. Engaging the private sector and enco
uraging public-
private partnerships can accelerate the adoption of these technologies
and drive significant reductions in emissions.

Adaptation

While mitigation efforts are essential for long-
term climate stability, adaptation is necessary to cope with the change
s that are already underway. In Florida, this means building resilience
into the very fabric of communities and infrastructure.

Urban planning and building codes must evolve to account for higher
sea levels and stronger storms. This includes constructing homes and
public buildings to withstand extreme weather, elevating structures in
flood-
prone areas, and incorporating green infrastructure to manage stormw
ater. Coastal communities, in particular, need robust defenses against
rising seas, such as seawalls, barrier islands, and restored wetlands tha
t can absorb storm surges.

Investment in resilient infrastructure extends to transportation and util
ities. Roads, bridges, and power grids must be fortified to endure mor
e frequent and severe weather events. For instance, burying power lin
es can reduce the risk of outages during hurricanes, and upgrading sto
rmwater systems can prevent flooding in urban areas.

Public education and community engagement are also critical. Ensuring that residents understand the risks associated with climate change and hurricanes, and know how to prepare and respond, can save lives and reduce property damage. This includes regular drills, clear communication from authorities, and accessible resources for emergency planning.

Finally, economic strategies must address the financial impacts of climate change. This involves creating insurance programs that can better cope with the increased risks, offering incentives for property owners to invest in resilience measures, and ensuring that low-income and vulnerable populations have the support they need to adapt.

CASE STUDIES: COMMUNITY RES ILIENCE AND REBUILDING

When a hurricane rips through a community, the aftermath is often as telling as the storm itself. The resilience and determination of those af fected define the path to recovery and rebuilding. Two notable case st udies, the rebirth of Homestead after Hurricane Andrew and the unite d response of Naples to Hurricane Irma, offer profound insights into t he power of community spirit and the complexities of recovery.

The Rebirth of Homestead Post-Andrew

Homestead, a city located in MiamiDade County, bore the brunt of H urricane Andrew's wrath in August 1992. The storm struck with such force that it left a landscape resembling a war zone. Homes were flatte ned, businesses destroyed, and lives upended in a matter of hours. An drew's winds, peaking at 165 mph, were relentless, and the damage w as catastrophic.

In the early aftermath, the community faced a formidable challenge.

The destruction was so severe that many wondered if Homestead cou ld ever fully recover. Yet, in the face of this adversity, a remarkable tr ansformation began. The people of Homestead, along with local and f ederal support, embarked on an arduous journey of rebuilding.

The response to Andrew underscored the importance of community re silience. Residents came together to support one another, sharing reso urces and providing emotional support. Volunteer organizations, chur ches, and civic groups played crucial roles in coordinating relief effort s, distributing food, and offering shelter to those who lost their homes. The sense of solidarity was palpable, and it became the foundation up on which the city's recovery was built.

Reconstruction efforts were swift but challenging. The widespread de struction meant that rebuilding had to start from scratch in many areas . However, this also provided an opportunity to improve infrastructure and building standards. The introduction of stricter building codes en sured that new structures would be more resilient to future storms. Th ese regulations required homes to be built to withstand higher wind sp eeds and mandated the use of stronger materials and better constructio n techniques.

Economic recovery was equally significant. The federal government p rovided substantial aid, and businesses gradually returned, creating jo bs and stimulating local economic activity. The presence of Homestea d Air Reserve Base, which also suffered extensive damage, played a c ritical role in the city's rebirth. Its rebuilding injected millions of dolla rs into the local economy and provided employment opportunities.

Over the years, Homestead's transformation has been nothing short of remarkable. The city not only rebuilt but also thrived, becoming a sy

mbol of resilience and determination. Its story serves as a powerful te
stament to the strength of community spirit and the importance of pre
paredness and adaptation in the face of natural disasters.

Naples and Irma: A Community United

Fast forward to 2017, when Hurricane Irma, one of the most powerful
 hurricanes ever recorded in the Atlantic, set its sights on Florida. Nap
les, a picturesque city on Florida's Gulf Coast, was directly in its path.
 As Irma approached, the community braced for impact, drawing on le
ssons learned from past storms and the collective will to face the chall
enge together.

Irma made landfall in Naples on September 10, 2017, as a Category 3
hurricane with winds of 115 mph. The storm brought significant dama
ge, flooding streets, knocking down power lines, and leaving thousan
ds without electricity. Trees were uprooted, homes were damaged, an
d businesses were forced to close. Yet, amid the chaos, the communit
y's response was swift and coordinated.

Local authorities, emergency responders, and utility companies had pr
epared extensively in the leadup to the storm. This preparation paid of
f, as power restoration efforts began almost immediately after Irma pa
ssed. The city's emergency management teams worked tirelessly to cl
ear debris and restore essential services. Volunteer organizations and l

ocal residents came together to assist those in need, providing food, w ater, and shelter.

One of the most inspiring aspects of Naples' recovery was the unity di splayed by its residents. Neighbors helped each other clear debris and repair damage. Social media platforms became vital communication t ools, allowing people to share information, seek help, and offer assista nce. The collective effort demonstrated the power of community and t he importance of working together in times of crisis.

Naples' experience with Hurricane Irma also highlighted the role of p roactive measures in enhancing resilience. The city had implemented flood mitigation projects, such as improved drainage systems, which h elped reduce the extent of flooding. Building codes had been updated to ensure that new constructions could withstand stronger storms, and public awareness campaigns had educated residents on hurricane prep aredness.

The economic impact of Irma was significant, particularly on the touri sm and real estate sectors, which are vital to Naples' economy. Howe ver, the city's resilience and the speed of recovery efforts helped miti gate longterm damage. Businesses reopened, tourists returned, and the real esta te market rebounded.

Naples' response to Hurricane Irma is a testament to the power of pre paredness, community spirit, and resilience. It illustrates how a united community can overcome immense challenges and emerge stronger. The lessons learned from Naples and Homestead provide valuable insi ghts for other communities facing similar threats, emphasizing the im portance of building resilience and fostering a sense of unity in the fac e of natural disasters.

Further Insights and Lessons

These case studies also highlight the importance of psychological resil ience. Posttraumatic stress disorder (PTSD) and other mental health is sues can emerge after such traumatic events. Community mental healt h services play a crucial role in helping residents cope and rebuild thei r lives emotionally and psychologically. Peer support groups, counseli ng services, and community events can foster a sense of normalcy and provide much-needed support.

The role of technology in disaster response has also become increasin gly significant. Advanced weather forecasting, realtime communicatio n platforms, and the use of drones for damage assessment have revolu tionized how communities prepare for and respond to hurricanes. The se technological advancements enable quicker, more efficient recover y efforts and better coordination among various stakeholders.

VOICES FROM THE STORM

Hurricanes have an uncanny ability to strip life down to its essentials, revealing raw human experiences in the face of nature's ferocity. The stories that emerge from these storms are often powerful, heartbreaking, and inspiring. They provide a deeply personal look at the impact of hurricanes, capturing moments of fear, courage, loss, and resilience. These voices from the storm are essential to understanding the full scope of a hurricane's impact beyond the statistics and headlines.

Personal Accounts and Eyewitness Testimonies

One of the most compelling aspects of hurricane stories is the first-hand accounts of those who lived through them. These personal narratives offer a glimpse into the chaos and emotional turbulence experienced during and after the storm.

Take, for instance, the story of Maria Hernandez, who survived Hurricane Andrew in 1992. Maria's family home in Homestead was reduced to rubble within hours. She recalls the deafening roar of the wind, the windows shattering, and the roof being torn off as she and her children huddled in the bathroom. "It felt like the world was ending," she says. Yet, in the aftermath, the community's spirit of solidarity and support gave her hope. Neighbors who had once been strangers shared food, water, and helped each other rebuild.

Another poignant testimony comes from Thomas Williams, a resident of Naples during Hurricane Irma in 2017. Thomas was among those who chose to stay and ride out the storm, a decision he describes as both terrifying and humbling. As the winds howled and the waters rose, he and his wife took refuge in their attic. "We thought we might not make it," he admits. But after the storm passed, Thomas emerged to find his community already coming together. People were clearing debris, checking on each other, and organizing relief efforts. His story reflects the incredible resilience and neighborly spirit that hurricanes often bring to the forefront.

Children, too, have vivid and unique perspectives on these events. Eight-year-old Chloe Martin's recounting of her experience during Hurricane Michael in 2018 is both heartbreaking and hopeful. She talks about the fear of losing her home and her pets but also about the joy of seeing her school friends helping to distribute food and supplies at the local shelter. Her childlike optimism and bravery offer a touching reminder of the human capacity to find light even in the darkest times.

These personal accounts not only humanize the impact of hurricanes but also serve as powerful testimonies of resilience and community spirit. They remind us that behind every statistic is a story of real people facing extraordinary challenges and coming together to overcome them.

The Role of Media in Shaping Public Perception

The media plays a pivotal role in shaping public perception of hurricanes, from the initial warnings and coverage of the storm to the post-event analysis and storytelling. The way these events are reported can influence public understanding, preparedness, and response.

During a hurricane, media outlets become lifelines of information. They provide critical updates on the storm's path, intensity, and safety measures. However, the responsibility of the media goes beyond just reporting; it involves conveying the urgency and seriousness of the situation without inciting undue panic. Balanced, factual reporting is crucial in ensuring that people take necessary precautions while maintaining a sense of calm.

In the aftermath, the media's role shifts to covering the impact and the recovery efforts. This coverage can highlight the areas most in need of aid, bringing national and international attention to the affected regions. The stories of heroism, generosity, and resilience that are featured can inspire public support and donations, as well as provide a sense of solidarity and hope to those directly affected.

However, media coverage is not without its challenges and criticisms. There is often debate about the balance between sensationalism and responsible journalism. Dramatic footage and headlines can draw viewers and readers, but they can also contribute to a sense of fear and helplessness. Moreover, there is the issue of coverage disparity wherein some communities, especially those less affluent or less well-known, receive less attention and aid.

Social media has added a new dimension to how hurricanes are reported and perceived. Platforms like Twitter, Facebook, and Instagram allow for real-time sharing of information and personal experiences. This democratization of reporting means that individuals can share their stories directly, offering raw, unfiltered insights. It also means that misinformation can spread quickly, making media literacy and critical evaluation skills more important than ever.

Furthermore, documentaries and investigative journalism often provide in-depth analyses and personal stories that might get lost in the immediate coverage of the storm. These long-form pieces can delve into the systemic issues that exacerbate the impact of hurricanes, such as inadequate infrastructure, socio-economic disparities, and environmental degradation. They also offer a platform for survivors to share their experiences in their own words, fostering a deeper understanding of the human side of these natural disasters.

POLICY AND PREPAREDNESS

Navigating the challenges posed by hurricanes requires more than just immediate disaster response; it demands comprehensive policy and p reparedness strategies that evolve with changing circumstances and le ssons learned from past storms. Over the decades, the approach to hur ricane preparedness has undergone significant evolution, driven by tec hnological advancements, shifts in policy, and the invaluable lessons gleaned from the aftermath of devastating hurricanes.

Evolution of Hurricane Preparedness Plans

In the early days of hurricane preparedness, the focus was primarily o n immediate response. Communities relied on basic weather forecasts and rudimentary warning systems. In the mid20th century, as meteoro logy advanced, the ability to predict hurricanes improved. The develo pment of the SaffirSimpson Hurricane Wind Scale in the 1970s provi ded a standardized way to convey the potential impact of hurricanes, helping communities better understand the risks.

However, it was the devastation wrought by Hurricane Andrew in 199 2 that marked a turning point. The sheer scale of destruction in South Florida exposed critical gaps in building codes, emergency response p rotocols, and public awareness. The state of Florida and federal agenc ies recognized the need for a more proactive and comprehensive appr oach to hurricane preparedness.

In response, building codes were significantly strengthened. New regu
lations required structures to be built to withstand higher wind speeds,
 with stricter standards for roofing, windows, and construction materia
ls. These changes aimed to reduce the vulnerability of buildings to hur
ricane-force winds and flying debris.

Emergency management also saw substantial advancements. The esta
blishment of the Federal Emergency Management Agency (FEMA) a
nd the enhancement of state and local emergency operations centers i
mproved coordination and communication during disasters. The imple
mentation of detailed evacuation plans, including the identification of
evacuation routes and the designation of shelters, became a priority.

Public awareness campaigns were launched to educate residents about
 hurricane preparedness. These campaigns emphasized the importance
 of having an emergency kit, creating a family communication plan, a
nd understanding evacuation procedures. The use of social media and
other digital platforms has further enhanced the dissemination of critic
al information, ensuring that communities are informed and prepared.

Additionally, regional collaborations have become a cornerstone of hu
rricane preparedness. States along the Gulf and Atlantic coasts have d
eveloped joint response strategies and resource-
sharing agreements. These cooperative efforts ensure that, when disas
ter strikes, there are ample resources and support systems in place to p
rovide timely aid and recovery efforts.

Lessons Learned and Future Directions

Every hurricane brings with it valuable lessons that shape future prepa redness and response strategies. Hurricane Katrina in 2005 underscore d the importance of addressing the needs of vulnerable populations, su ch as the elderly, disabled, and lowincome residents, who may face gr eater challenges during evacuations and recovery.

The impact of Hurricane Sandy in 2012 highlighted the need for resili ent infrastructure. In response, efforts to upgrade aging infrastructure, including power grids and transportation networks, have intensified. Coastal cities have invested in flood barriers, seawalls, and improved drainage systems to mitigate the effects of storm surges and flooding.

Climate change has added a new layer of complexity to hurricane pre paredness. Rising sea levels and increasing ocean temperatures are ex pected to lead to more frequent and intense hurricanes. This reality ne cessitates a forward-looking approach to preparedness and policy.

Future directions in hurricane preparedness involve a combination of t echnological innovation, policy adjustments, and community engage ment. Here are some key areas of focus:

1. **Advanced Forecasting and Early Warning Systems**: Continuou s advancements in meteorology and technology are improving the accuracy of hurricane forecasts. The development of more sophisti cated models and the use of artificial intelligence can enhance the

ability to predict storm intensity and track changes in real-time, providing communities with better early warnings.

2. **Resilient Infrastructure**: Building infrastructure that can withstand extreme weather events is paramount. This includes not only homes and buildings but also critical infrastructure such as roads, bridges, and power systems. Investments in green infrastructure, like wetlands and mangroves, can provide natural buffers against storm surges.

3. **CommunityBased Approaches**: Empowering communities to take an active role in preparedness is essential. Local governments, community organizations, and residents must collaborate to develop tailored preparedness plans that address specific local risks. Public education campaigns should be ongoing, ensuring that residents remain vigilant and prepared.

4. **Policy and Regulation**: Policymakers must continue to refine regulations that enhance building standards and landuse planning. Incentives for property owners to retrofit existing structures to meet higher resilience standards can also be effective. Additionally, policies should address the needs of vulnerable populations, ensuring that they have access to resources and support during and after hurricanes.

5. **Global Collaboration**: Hurricanes are a global phenomenon, and collaboration between countries can enhance preparedness efforts.

Sharing data, research, and best practices can lead to more effecti ve strategies worldwide. International cooperation can also facilita te rapid response and recovery efforts in the aftermath of major hu rricanes.

6. **Sustainable Practices**: Integrating sustainability into hurricane pr eparedness can yield longterm benefits. Reducing carbon emission s and promoting renewable energy sources can mitigate the impact s of climate change, ultimately reducing the frequency and intensit y of hurricanes.

Furthermore, integrating psychological preparedness into emergency plans is gaining recognition. Mental health professionals advocate for the inclusion of psychological first aid in disaster response, ensuring t hat individuals and communities have access to mental health support during and after hurricanes. This holistic approach to preparedness ac knowledges that emotional resilience is just as critical as physical safe ty.

THE WAY FORWARD

The frequency and intensity of hurricanes impacting Florida are on an upward trend, spurred by the inexorable march of climate change. As these storms grow stronger and more unpredictable, the need for inno vative solutions becomes increasingly urgent. The path forward lies in harnessing the power of technology and embracing a culture of resilie nce. Florida, with its unique vulnerabilities and strengths, stands at the forefront of this battle, striving to protect its people, economy, and na tural beauty.

Technology and Innovation in Hurricane Prediction

Accurate hurricane prediction is the cornerstone of effective prepared ness and response. Over the past decades, advancements in technolog y have significantly improved our ability to predict hurricanes, but the journey is far from over. The future of hurricane prediction lies in lev eraging cuttingedge technology to provide even more precise and time ly forecasts.

One of the most promising advancements is the integration of artificia l intelligence (AI) and machine learning into meteorological models. These technologies can analyze vast amounts of data from satellites, weather stations, and ocean buoys to identify patterns and predict stor m behavior with greater accuracy. AI can also help forecasters underst and the factors that lead to rapid intensification, a phenomenon that has caught many by surprise in recent years.

Another critical innovation is the use of drones and unmanned aerial vehicles (UAVs) for data collection. These devices can fly into the heart of a storm, collecting realtime data on wind speeds, pressure, and temperature. This information is invaluable for improving models and providing up-to-the-
minute updates. Drones can also be deployed after hurricanes to assess damage and assist in search and rescue operations, speeding up the response time and saving lives.

Satellite technology continues to play a vital role in hurricane prediction. Advances in satellite imaging and remote sensing allow for continuous monitoring of weather systems. The latest generation of satellites can provide highresolution images and detailed data on storm formation and movement, enhancing our ability to track hurricanes from their inception.
Supercomputing is another gamechanger in the field of meteorology. Highperformance computing systems can process complex models and simulations at incredible speeds, enabling forecasters to run multiple scenarios and predict potential storm paths more accurately. These simulations take into account a wide range of variables, including sea surface temperatures, atmospheric conditions, and topography, to provi

de a comprehensive picture of a storm's trajectory and potential impa
ct.

Collaboration between international meteorological agencies is also es
sential. Hurricanes are not confined to national borders, and sharing d
ata and expertise can enhance global preparedness. Joint initiatives, su
ch as the World Meteorological Organization's Hurricane Committee,
facilitate the exchange of information and best practices, ensuring tha
t all nations are better equipped to handle these powerful storms.

Building a Resilient Florida

As hurricane prediction technology advances, the focus must also be o
n building a resilient Florida. Resilience is not just about bouncing ba
ck from disasters; it's about being prepared, adaptable, and sustainabl
e in the face of future threats.

Urban planning and development play a crucial role in building resilie
nce. Coastal cities must adopt smart growth strategies that minimize v
ulnerability to hurricanes. This includes implementing stricter buildin
g codes, designing floodresistant infrastructure, and preserving natural
buffers like wetlands and mangroves. Green infrastructure, such as
rain gardens and permeable pavements, can assist manage stormwater
and lessen the danger of flooding.

Community engagement is another cornerstone of resilience. Educatin
g residents about hurricane preparedness and involving them in planni

ng efforts can empower communities to take proactive measures. Publ ic awareness campaigns should emphasize the importance of having a n emergency plan, securing property, and knowing evacuation routes. Community drills and training sessions can also enhance preparedness and ensure that everyone knows what to do when a hurricane strikes.

Investment in resilient infrastructure is critical. This means not only re pairing and upgrading existing infrastructure but also designing new p rojects with future risks in mind. For instance, elevating roads and bri dges, reinforcing seawalls, and installing flood barriers can provide vi tal protection against storm surges and rising sea levels. Utility compa nies should invest in underground power lines and robust grid systems to minimize disruptions during hurricanes.

Economic resilience is equally important. The state must support busi nesses in developing continuity plans and provide resources for small businesses to recover quickly after a storm. Diversifying the economy and promoting industries that are less vulnerable to hurricanes, such a s technology and renewable energy, can also strengthen economic resi lience.

Additionally, social resilience must be prioritized. Vulnerable populat ions, including the elderly, disabled, and lowincome residents, need ta rgeted support to ensure they can withstand and recover from hurrican es. This includes access to affordable housing, healthcare, and social s ervices. Building strong social networks and fostering a sense of com

munity can also enhance resilience, as people come together to suppor
t each other in times of need.

Looking to the future, Florida must embrace sustainability as a core pr
inciple of resilience. Reducing greenhouse gas emissions, promoting r
enewable energy, and protecting natural ecosystems are essential step
s in mitigating the longterm impacts of climate change. Sustainable pr
actices not only reduce the state's carbon footprint but also create a he
althier, more resilient environment for future generations.

Enhanced communication networks are vital in ensuring timely disse
mination of information before, during, and after hurricanes. Leveragi
ng 5G technology can provide faster and more reliable communicatio
n, essential for coordinating emergency response efforts and keeping t
he public informed. Mobile apps and platforms can offer real-
time updates, evacuation alerts, and resources, making crucial informa
tion accessible to all residents.

Incorporating traditional ecological knowledge and practices can also
bolster resilience. Indigenous communities have a deep understanding
 of local ecosystems and historical weather patterns. Engaging these c
ommunities in planning and decisionmaking processes can provide va
luable insights and foster inclusive approaches to resilience.

Research and innovation must continue to drive advancements in buil
ding materials and construction techniques. Developing materials that
are more resistant to wind, water, and debris impact can enhance the d

urability of infrastructure. Innovations such as selfhealing materials, which can repair minor damage over time, and modular construction, which allows for quicker and more flexible rebuilding, can revolutioni ze the way we approach hurricane resilience.

Publicprivate partnerships can amplify efforts to build a resilient Flori da. Collaboration between government agencies, private companies, a nd nonprofit organizations can pool resources, expertise, and technolo gy to create comprehensive solutions. For instance, tech companies ca n work with municipalities to develop smart city initiatives that enhan ce real-time monitoring and response capabilities.

CONCLUSION

Reflecting on a century of storms in Florida reveals a tapestry woven with tales of resilience, lessons learned, and enduring legacies. Hurric anes have been both a bane and a catalyst for change, shaping the stat e's policies, infrastructure, and community spirit in profound ways. As we look back, it's clear that each storm has left an indelible mark, and the collective experiences have fostered a more prepared and resilient Florida.

The history of hurricanes in Florida is a testament to the formidable fo rce of nature and the enduring spirit of its residents. From the early 20 th century storms to the modernday hurricanes, each event has impart ed valuable lessons and left behind legacies that continue to influence the state's approach to disaster preparedness and response.

One of the most significant lessons gleaned from a century of hurrican es is the importance of robust and resilient infrastructure. The devastat ion of Hurricane Andrew in 1992 exposed the vulnerabilities in buildi ng codes and construction practices. In response, Florida implemented stringent building regulations that required structures to withstand hig her wind speeds and impacts. These changes have undoubtedly saved lives and reduced property damage in subsequent storms.

Another crucial lesson is the need for comprehensive emergency man agement and preparedness plans. The chaotic response to Hurricane A

ndrew highlighted the gaps in coordination and communication amon
g federal, state, and local agencies. Since then, the establishment of th
e Federal Emergency Management Agency (FEMA) and the enhance
ment of state and local emergency operations centers have significantl
y improved disaster response capabilities. Detailed evacuation plans,
pre-storm preparations, and post-
storm recovery efforts are now more organized and effective, ensurin
g that communities receive timely assistance.

Public awareness and education have also emerged as vital componen
ts of hurricane preparedness. Campaigns to inform residents about the
 importance of having an emergency kit, creating a family communica
tion plan, and knowing evacuation routes have become standard practi
ce. Social media and digital platforms play a critical role in dissemina
ting real-
time information, enabling residents to make informed decisions befor
e, during, and after a storm.

The significance of community resilience cannot be overstated. Hurric
anes have a unique way of bringing people together, fostering a sense
of solidarity and mutual support. Stories of neighbors helping each ot
her, volunteers providing aid, and local organizations stepping up to c
oordinate relief efforts are common in the aftermath of storms. This se
nse of community spirit has been instrumental in the recovery and reb
uilding process, highlighting the power of collective action.

The legacies of Florida's hurricanes are visible in its enhanced infrastr ucture, improved policies, and resilient communities. The stricter buil ding codes and construction practices that emerged after Hurricane A ndrew serve as a lasting legacy, ensuring that new structures are better equipped to withstand the forces of nature.

Emergency management policies have evolved, with a focus on proac tive measures and longterm recovery. The integration of climate chan ge considerations into disaster planning is a significant development, acknowledging the increasing frequency and intensity of hurricanes. I nitiatives to protect and restore natural buffers, such as wetlands and mangroves, are part of this legacy, providing both ecological benefits and additional protection against storm surges.

Technological advancements in hurricane prediction and tracking are another enduring legacy. The use of satellites, drones, and supercomp uters has revolutionized meteorology, allowing for more accurate fore casts and timely warnings. These innovations have undoubtedly saved lives by giving residents more time to prepare and evacuate if necess ary.

The economic landscape of Florida has also been shaped by its hurric ane history. The tourism and real estate industries, which are vital to t he state's economy, have adapted to the challenges posed by hurrican es. Investments in resilient infrastructure and marketing campaigns th at promote recovery and renewal have helped maintain Florida's appe al as a destination. The insurance industry, too, has evolved, with mor e sophisticated risk assessment models and coverage options designed to address the unique challenges posed by hurricanes.

On a social level, the legacy of community resilience and solidarity is perhaps the most enduring. The shared experiences of surviving and r ecovering from hurricanes have fostered a culture of preparedness and mutual support.

Community networks, volunteer organizations, and local leaders play a crucial role in ensuring that residents are equipped to handle future storms.

As we reflect on the past century of hurricanes in Florida, it's evident t hat the lessons learned have paved the way for a more resilient future. However, the journey is far from over. Climate change continues to p ose new challenges, with rising sea levels and increasing storm intensi ty necessitating ongoing adaptation and innovation.

The way forward requires a continued commitment to building resilie nce at all levelsindividual, community, and governmental. Embracing sustainable practices, investing in resilient infrastructure, and fosterin g a culture of preparedness and solidarity will be essential in navigatin g the challenges ahead.